WALKING
IN THE LIGHT

A 50-DAY EASTER DEVOTIONAL

Daily Reflections and Prayers
to Walk with Christ from
Resurrection to Pentecost

THOMAS KNIGHT

ISBN eBook: 978-1-961963-57-3
ISBN Paperback: 978-1-961963-58-0

Contact: info@chapterzerobooks.com

Contents

"All of them were filled with the Holy Spirit and began to speak in other tongues as the Spirit gave them utterance." — Acts 2:4

Introduction

"But if we walk in the light, as he is in the light, we have fellowship with one another, and the blood of Jesus his Son cleanses us from all sin." — 1 John 1:7

E aster is not just a moment in time; it is an invitation to walk in the light of Christ every single day. Too often, we celebrate the joy of the Resurrection on Easter Sunday, only to slip back into old routines, as if nothing has changed. But everything has changed. Jesus has conquered sin and death, and His victory is meant to shape our lives—not just for a day, but for a lifetime.

For fifty days, from the Resurrection to Pentecost, the Church calls us to dwell in this light—to let it illuminate our hearts, transform our minds, and guide our steps. This is a season of renewal, a time to deepen our faith and embrace the fullness of life that Jesus offers.

This devotional is designed to help you stay connected to the power of Easter, even as the world moves on. Each day will invite you to:

- Reflect on Scripture and the journey from Easter to Pentecost,

- Grow in faith through daily meditations on Christ's victory,

- Pray with intention, seeking His presence in your life,

- Live the Resurrection through small, meaningful actions.

As you begin this journey, know that you are not walking alone. Christ walks with you. His light is always shining, always calling, always leading you closer to Him.

So take a deep breath. Step into the light. Let these next fifty days be a time of transformation.

Let's begin.

Thomas Knight

CHAPTER ONE

Week 1 – The Light of the Resurrection

LIVING IN THE REALITY OF EASTER

Darkness was defeated the moment Christ stepped out of the tomb. But Easter is not just a story of an empty grave—it is an invitation to walk in His light. The Resurrection changes everything, and yet, too often, we live as if we are still in the shadows.

This week, we begin a journey of stepping fully into the light of Christ. Not just seeing it, but walking in it—letting His victory reshape our hearts, our vision, and our way of living. The light has come. Now, it's time to follow where it leads.

Day 1 - Step Into the Light

"But if we walk in the light, as he is in the light, we have fellowship with one another, and the blood of Jesus his Son cleanses us from all sin." — 1 John 1:7

＊＊＊

Easter morning changed everything. The stone was rolled away, the tomb was empty, and the risen Christ stepped into the light of a new day. In that moment, darkness lost its power, and the light of God's love shone in its fullness.

But Easter is not just about what happened to Jesus—it's about what happens to us. His Resurrection is an invitation to step into that same light, leaving behind the shadows of sin, doubt, and fear. Too often, we hesitate. We stay in familiar places, afraid to fully embrace the transformation Christ offers.

John reminds us that walking in the light is not just about personal faith—it's about fellowship. When we choose to live in Christ's light, we are drawn closer to Him and to one another. The Resurrection calls us not only to believe in the risen Christ but to live in His light daily—a light that brings healing, renewal, and deep, lasting joy.

What does it mean for you to step into the light today? What shadows are you still clinging to?

＊＊＊

Jesus,
You are the light that no darkness can overcome.

Help me to walk in Your light today,
leaving behind fear, doubt,
and anything that keeps me
from fully embracing Your victory.
Let Your presence shine in my heart,
guiding my steps and deepening my fellowship
with You and others. Amen.

Spend a few moments in prayer today, asking God to reveal any areas of your life where you are still walking in the shadows. Write down one step you can take to embrace His light more fully.

Day 2: The Light That Leads

"Again Jesus spoke to them, saying, 'I am the light of the world. Whoever follows me will not walk in darkness, but will have the light of life.'" — John 8:12

Jesus tells us that following Him means leaving behind the darkness—not just the darkness of sin, but the darkness of uncertainty, fear, and self-reliance. Walking in His light doesn't mean we will always see the full path ahead. Sometimes, it's just enough light for the next step.

Maybe today, you feel unsure about the road before you. Maybe you long for clarity, for certainty. Jesus doesn't promise to show us every detail of the journey, but He does promise that when we follow Him, we will never walk in darkness. His light will always be enough.

Where do you need to trust His light today? What step is He asking you to take?

Jesus, You are the light of the world.
Help me to trust You
even when I don't see the full picture.
Lead me in Your truth and teach me
to walk in Your light, one step at a time.
May I follow You with faith,
knowing that Your light will never fail me. Amen.

Think about one area of your life where you feel uncertain or afraid. Spend a few moments in quiet prayer, asking Jesus to guide you. Write down one practical way you can trust His light today.

Day 3: Recognizing Jesus in Everyday Life

"When he was at the table with them, he took the bread and blessed and broke it and gave it to them. And their eyes were opened, and they recognized him." — Luke 24:30-31

The road to Emmaus was long, and the two disciples walked it with heavy hearts. They had heard the news of the empty tomb, yet they did not fully believe. Their minds were clouded by sorrow, and even as Jesus walked beside them, they failed to recognize Him.

How often do we do the same? We search for Jesus in big, miraculous moments, expecting a grand display of His presence. But more often than not, He meets us in the ordinary—in a quiet prayer, in the kindness of a stranger, in the breaking of bread.

It wasn't until Jesus took the bread, blessed it, and broke it that their eyes were opened. He had been with them all along. Could it be that He has been with you, too, in ways you have not yet recognized?

Take a moment today to reflect: Where might Jesus be walking with you in ways you haven't noticed?

Jesus,
open my eyes to Your presence in my daily life.
Help me not to overlook the ways
You are near—through simple moments,
through people around me,

through Your quiet whisper in my heart.
Give me a heart that sees
and a faith that trusts,
even when I do not understand. Amen.

———◄O►———

Pay attention today. Whether in a conversation, a small act of kindness, or a moment of peace, be intentional about looking for signs of Jesus' presence. Write down one moment where you sense God near.

Day 4: Called Out of Darkness

"You are a chosen people, a royal priesthood, a holy nation, God's special possession, that you may declare the praises of him who called you out of darkness into his wonderful light."
— 1 Peter 2:9

———◄O►———

The Resurrection of Jesus was not just a victory over death—it was an invitation into new life. Through Him, we are no longer defined by sin, failure, or the darkness of our past. We are called into His wonderful light, set apart as His people, meant to live in the fullness of His grace.

But stepping into the light requires something from us. It means leaving behind the old self—the doubts that hold us back, the fears that keep us from trusting God fully, the habits that pull us away from Him. It is a daily choice to live as people redeemed by Christ, rather than as those still bound by the past.

Peter reminds us that we are chosen, not forgotten. We belong to God, and we have been given a purpose: to declare His praises, to live as witnesses of His light. The empty tomb was not the end of the story—it was the beginning of a life that shines with the radiance of Christ.

Where is God calling you to step out of darkness today? What part of your life needs to be surrendered to His light?

Father, thank You for calling me into Your light.
Help me to leave behind everything
that keeps me from fully living
in the truth of Your love.
May my life reflect Your glory,
and may I walk in the freedom
You have given me. Amen.

Identify one area of your life where you still struggle with "old ways"—a habit, a fear, a mindset. Ask God to help you step into His light in that area today.

Day 5: Walking as Children of Light

"For at one time you were darkness, but now you are light in the Lord. Walk as children of light." — Ephesians 5:8

———◦———

Easter is not just about celebrating that Jesus is risen—it's about living as people transformed by His Resurrection. Paul reminds us that we were once in darkness, but through Christ, we have been made light. That's a powerful statement. Not just that we walk in the light, but that we are light in the Lord.

Yet, how often do we forget this? We let worry cloud our faith, we hold on to past failures, we hesitate to fully trust God's plans. But if we are children of light, then our lives should reflect the reality of the Resurrection—not just on Easter Sunday, but every day.

Walking as children of light means:

- Choosing truth over fear.

- Living with faith, not anxiety.

- Letting God's love shine through our words and actions.

It doesn't mean we are perfect. It means we allow Christ to shine through us, guiding our steps and shaping our hearts.

Where is God asking you to walk as a child of light today?

———◦———

Jesus, You have made me light in You.
Help me to live in a way that reflects
Your love, Your truth, and Your power.
Let me walk with confidence,
knowing that Your light is within me. Amen.

———◆◇◆———

Be intentional today about reflecting Christ's light. Show kindness, speak encouragement, or choose faith over fear in a difficult moment. At the end of the day, reflect: Where did I walk as a child of light?

Day 6: A Light That Cannot Be Hidden

"You are the light of the world. A city set on a hill cannot be hidden." — Matthew 5:14

———◆◇◆———

The Resurrection was never meant to be a private event. Jesus rose from the grave so that the whole world would know that death had been defeated and that His light would never be overcome. And now, He turns to us and says: "You are the light of the world."

It's a remarkable statement. Jesus, the Light of the world, calls us to be His light-bearers. Not because we are perfect or without flaws, but because His victory has become our own. Yet, how often do we hesitate? How often do we shrink back in fear or stay silent when we should speak of His goodness?

A city on a hill cannot be hidden. Light does not try to hide; it shines because that is its nature. When Christ's light fills us, we are not meant to keep it to ourselves. It should be evident in the way we love, in the way we forgive, in the way we live as people who have been redeemed.

The world needs this light. The people around you need it. Not a forced or artificial light, but the genuine glow of someone who has encountered the risen Christ and been changed by Him.

What would it look like for you to live unafraid, fully embracing the light Jesus has placed within you?

Jesus, You have called me
to shine with Your light.
Remove anything in me that dims that light
—fear, doubt, hesitation.
Help me to live boldly for You,
that others may see Your love
and be drawn to You. Amen.

Be mindful today of moments when you might hesitate to show Christ's light—whether in kindness, courage, or truth. Choose to shine, even in small ways.

Day 7: The Light That Transforms

"And we all, who with unveiled faces contemplate the Lord's glory, are being transformed into his image with ever-increasing glory, which comes from the Lord, who is the Spirit." — 2 Corinthians 3:18

When Jesus rose from the dead, He didn't just prove His power over death—He made a way for our transformation. The Resurrection is not just an event we celebrate; it is a reality that is meant to change us, shaping us more and more into the image of Christ.

Paul describes this as a process of "ever-increasing glory." The more we seek Jesus, the more His light shines in us. It's not about striving to be perfect, but about being willing to be changed, to let go of what holds us back, and to allow His Spirit to renew us day by day.

But transformation requires openness. When Moses encountered the presence of God, his face shone with divine radiance—but he veiled it before the people. Paul reminds us that in Christ, the veil is removed. We are invited to stand fully in His presence, to be shaped by His love, and to reflect His light without fear.

Where is God calling you to be transformed? What part of your heart still resists His light? The beauty of the Resurrection is that we are never left as we were—we are always being made new.

Jesus,
I open my heart to Your transforming light.
Remove anything in me
that resists Your work.
Let me reflect Your love
more and more each day,
growing in faith and walking in Your presence.
Amen.

———◄O►———

Spend a few quiet moments in prayer today. Ask God to reveal an area where He wants to bring transformation in your life. Trust that He is at work in you, even when you can't see it.

MY NOTES

MY NOTES

CHAPTER TWO

Week 2 – Walking in New Life

LIVING AS A NEW CREATION IN CHRIST

Resurrection is not just about leaving the grave behind—it's about stepping into something new. Christ didn't rise to restore the old, but to bring forth a transformed life.

This week, we embrace what it means to be made new. Not just forgiven, but renewed. Not just changed, but changed from the inside out. The past no longer defines us. The power of the risen Christ is at work within us. It's time to live as who we truly are in Him.

Day 8: Made New in Christ

"Therefore, if anyone is in Christ, he is a new creation. The old has passed away; behold, the new has come." — 2 Corinthians
5:17

The Resurrection was not just a moment in history—it was the beginning of something entirely new. Jesus did not rise from the grave to return to life as it was before. He stepped into a new kind of life, a glorified existence that would never again be touched by death. And He invites us into that same renewal.

Paul's words remind us that being in Christ changes everything. The old self—the one weighed down by sin, doubt, and fear—has passed away. In its place, something new is born. Yet, even though we are made new in Christ, we often find ourselves clinging to the old. We hesitate to let go of past mistakes, old habits, or limiting beliefs that keep us from fully embracing who we are in Him.

New life in Christ is not about striving—it's about receiving. It's about believing that His work is enough, that we don't have to carry the weight of what was, because He has already carried it to the cross.

Today, pause and ask yourself: Am I living as a new creation, or am I still holding onto the old?

———◆◇◆———

Jesus,
You have made me new.
Help me to step fully into the life You have given me,
leaving behind the burdens of my past.
Teach me to trust in Your transforming power

and to walk forward in the freedom of Your grace.

Amen.

———◄◙►———

Take a moment to reflect: Is there something from your past—guilt, fear, doubt—that you are still carrying? Write it down, and in prayer, surrender it to Jesus, trusting that He has already made you new.

Day 9: Leaving the Grave Behind

"Jesus said to her, 'Do not hold on to me, for I have not yet ascended to the Father. But go to my brothers and tell them, "I am ascending to my Father and your Father, to my God and your God."' — John 20:17

On the morning of the Resurrection, Mary Magdalene stood outside the empty tomb, weeping. She had come looking for Jesus, but when she saw Him standing before her, she did not recognize Him at first. Only when He spoke her name did she realize the truth—He was alive.

Her immediate reaction was to cling to Him, to hold onto the Jesus she had known before the cross. But Jesus gently told her, *"Do not hold on to me."* He was inviting her into something greater: a new way of knowing Him, a new reality where the Resurrection had changed everything.

How often do we try to hold on to what feels familiar, even when God is calling us forward? We may long for the comfort of the past, but Jesus is inviting us to step into the new life He has prepared. The grave is empty—not just His, but ours, too. Whatever has been holding us back—guilt, fear, doubt—has no place in the resurrected life.

Mary was not meant to stay at the tomb. She was meant to go and tell, to step forward into her calling. And so are we.

Is there something from your past you are holding onto, something Jesus is calling you to release so you can fully embrace the life He has for you?

Jesus,
I don't want to stay at the grave
when You are calling me forward.
Help me to trust that the new life You offer
is better than anything I leave behind.
Give me the faith to let go
and step into Your resurrection power.
Amen.

Spend time in prayer today, asking God to reveal anything you are clinging to that is keeping you from moving forward. Ask Him for the courage to release it and embrace His new life for you.

Day 10: Set Free to Walk in Grace

"So if the Son sets you free, you will be free indeed." — John
8:36

Freedom is one of the greatest gifts of the Resurrection. Jesus didn't just defeat death—He broke every chain that bound us. Yet, many of us still live as though we are captive. We hold onto guilt that He has already forgiven, carry burdens He has already lifted, and live in fear when He has already secured our victory.

Think of Lazarus. When Jesus called him out of the tomb, he was alive, but still wrapped in grave clothes. Jesus told those around him, *"Unbind him, and let him go."* (John 11:44). New life had already been given, but the remnants of death still clung to him.

We are often the same way. Jesus has called us into a new life of grace, yet we sometimes keep the old wrappings—old habits, shame, or self-doubt. But if the Son has set us free, then we are free indeed. Not partially free, not conditionally free—fully, completely free.

Today, choose to walk in that freedom. Let go of whatever is holding you back from fully embracing who you are in Christ. The grave is empty. The chains are broken. You are free.

What are you still carrying that Jesus has already taken from you?

———◄O►———

Jesus,
You have set me free.
Help me to live in the truth of that freedom,
leaving behind the chains of the past.
Teach me to walk in Your grace,

unburdened and unafraid.

Amen.

———◆◇◆———

Take a moment to reflect on an area where you still feel "bound." Ask Jesus to unbind you and help you walk forward in His grace. Write down a declaration of freedom based on today's scripture.

Day 11: Clothed in Christ

"For all of you who were baptized into Christ have clothed yourselves with Christ." — Galatians 3:27

When you wake up in the morning, one of the first things you do is choose what to wear. Clothing not only protects us but also represents something about who we are. Paul uses this image to remind us that, in Christ, we have been given a new identity—and we are called to wear it.

The Resurrection is not just about leaving behind the old; it's about putting on the new. In baptism, we are wrapped in Christ, no longer defined by past failures or insecurities. His righteousness becomes ours, His grace covers us, His love becomes the foundation of who we are.

But just like we choose our clothing each day, we must also choose daily to walk in this identity. We can either wear the truth of who Christ says we are—redeemed, loved, and chosen—or we can put back on the garments of our old selves—shame, doubt, and fear.

What are you clothing yourself with today? Are you wearing the confidence of someone loved by God, or are you still carrying the weight of an identity Jesus already freed you from?

———◆◆———

Jesus,
I want to be clothed in You.
Help me to set aside anything that keeps me
from embracingmy identity as Your beloved.
Let me walk in the confidence
of being wrapped in Your grace.
Amen.

———◆◆———

As you get dressed today, take a moment to reflect on what it means to be "clothed in Christ." Ask yourself: Am I living as someone who belongs fully to Him? What old identity do I need to let go of?

Day 12: Strengthened by His Grace

"But he said to me, 'My grace is sufficient for you, for my power is made perfect in weakness.' Therefore I will boast all the more gladly of my weaknesses, so that the power of Christ may rest upon me." — 2 Corinthians 12:9

Living as a new creation doesn't mean we are suddenly perfect. We still stumble, we still struggle, and sometimes we feel like we aren't changing fast enough. But Jesus reminds us that His grace is enough.

Paul, one of the greatest messengers of the gospel, pleaded with God to take away his struggles. Yet God didn't remove them—instead, He revealed that grace is not about our strength, but His. When we feel weak, unworthy, or unable to move forward, that is exactly where His power shines the brightest.

Being transformed by Christ isn't about never failing—it's about leaning on His grace every single day. It's about realizing that we don't have to be perfect to be loved, we don't have to have it all figured out to walk in His light. His strength fills the spaces where we fall short.

Today, instead of being frustrated with your weaknesses, offer them to Jesus. Let His grace be enough.

———◄O►———

Jesus, I thank You
that I don't have to rely on my own strength.
When I feel weak, remind me
that Your grace is always enough.
Help me to trust that You are working in me,
even when I don't see it.
Amen.

———◄O►———

Think of one area where you feel weak or not "good enough." Instead of trying to fix it on your own, surrender it to Jesus. Write a prayer asking Him to show His strength in that area.

Day 13: Walking in the Spirit

"Since we live by the Spirit, let us keep in step with the Spirit." — Galatians 5:25

New life in Christ is not something we achieve on our own—it is the work of the Holy Spirit within us. When we surrender to Jesus, we are not just forgiven; we are given His Spirit to guide, strengthen, and transform us.

But walking in the Spirit is a daily choice. Paul reminds us that if we live by the Spirit, we must also keep in step with Him. This means learning to listen, to slow down, to follow His leading rather than rushing ahead with our own plans. It means trusting that even when we don't see immediate change, God is still at work.

Transformation is not just about what we do—it's about who we walk with. The Spirit is already in us, working, shaping, renewing. Our job is not to strive but to stay close to Him, allowing Him to lead us forward.

Are you keeping in step with the Spirit, or are you trying to move ahead on your own? What would it look like to let Him lead you today?

Holy Spirit,
help me to walk in step with You today.
Teach me to listen for Your voice,
to trust Your guidance,
and to rest in Your power.
Transform me from within
so that my life reflects
the new creation I am in Christ.
Amen.

———————◆◇◆———————

Take a moment today to pause and ask the Holy Spirit to guide you. Before making a decision—big or small—pray: *"Holy Spirit, lead me."* Notice how He speaks to your heart throughout the day.

Day 14: Bearing the Fruit of New Life

"I am the vine; you are the branches. If you remain in me and I in you, you will bear much fruit; apart from me you can do nothing." — John 15:5

When a branch is connected to the vine, it doesn't have to strive to produce fruit—it simply receives what it needs from the source. Jesus tells us that our new life in Him works the same way. When we remain in Him, His life flows through us, and transformation happens naturally.

But how often do we try to bear fruit on our own? We exhaust ourselves trying to be "better Christians," trying to change ourselves without relying on His strength. Yet Jesus reminds us: apart from Him, we can do nothing. It's not about pushing harder—it's about staying connected.

New life in Christ is not about effort, but about abiding. As we draw near to Him, His Spirit produces the fruit of love, joy, peace, patience, and all the evidence of a life changed by grace.

Are you abiding in Him, or are you trying to produce fruit on your own? What would it look like to simply receive His life today?

———◈———

Jesus,
I want to remain in You.
Help me to stop striving
and instead rest in Your presence,
trusting that You are at work in me.
Let my life bear fruit
that reflects Your love and truth.
Amen.

———◈———

Spend time in quiet reflection today. Instead of asking God to "fix" or "change" something in you, simply sit in His presence and ask Him to fill you with His Spirit. Trust that He is already working.

MY NOTES

MY NOTES

CHAPTER THREE

Week 3 – The Call to Witness

REFLECTING THE RESURRECTION OUTWARDLY

The light of the Resurrection was never meant to be hidden. What Christ has done in us is meant to shine through us.

This week, we step into our calling as witnesses—not by striving, but by reflecting the reality of His presence in our lives. To witness is not just to speak; it is to live in such a way that others see Jesus through us. The world needs the hope we have found. Will we let it be seen?

———◆———

Day 15: You Are His Witness

"You will receive power when the Holy Spirit comes on you; and you will be my witnesses in Jerusalem, and in all Judea and Samaria, and to the ends of the earth." — Acts 1:8

Before ascending into heaven, Jesus left His disciples with a clear calling: to be His witnesses. But notice what He says first—*"You will receive power."* He didn't ask them to go out on their own. He promised that the Holy Spirit would equip them for the mission.

Sometimes, we hesitate to share our faith because we feel unqualified or afraid of saying the wrong thing. But being a witness is not about having perfect words or knowledge—it's about testifying to what we have personally experienced. The disciples didn't go out proclaiming complex theology; they simply shared the truth that they had encountered the risen Christ.

Being a witness starts with living a life that reflects the reality of Jesus. It's in the way we love, the way we forgive, the way we extend grace. People don't just listen to what we say—they see how we live.

Where is God calling you to be a witness today? Who in your life needs to see the love of Jesus through you?

———— ◆◇◆ ————

Jesus,
You have called me to be Your witness,
but I often feel unworthy or afraid.
Remind me that I don't have to do this alone.
Fill me with Your Spirit so that my life

—through words, actions, and love—
points others to You. Amen.

———————◆◆◇◆◆———————

Identify one person in your life who may need encouragement or a reminder of God's love. Reach out to them today—with a word, an act of kindness, or a prayer. Trust that the Spirit is working through you.

Day 16: Light for the World

"Let your light shine before others, that they may see your good deeds and glorify your Father in heaven." — Matthew 5:16

The Resurrection didn't just change the lives of the disciples—it ignited a light that would spread across the world. Jesus calls us to be part of that light. He doesn't say, *"Try to shine"* or *"Work hard to be a light."* He simply says, *"You are the light of the world."*

But light is only effective when it's visible. A lamp hidden under a basket doesn't brighten a room. A city on a hill can't be ignored. The same is true for our faith—if we've been transformed by Christ, our lives should reflect it.

This doesn't mean drawing attention to ourselves. It means living in such a way that others see Christ through us—in our love, our kindness, our grace. Our witness is not just in the words we speak but in the way we forgive, serve, and show compassion. When people look at your life, do they see His light?

The world needs the light of Christ. And today, He is shining through you.

Jesus,
You have called me to shine with Your light.
Help me to live in a way that points others to You
—not by my strength, but by Your love within me.
Let everything I do today reflect Your presence.
Amen.

Be intentional today about shining Christ's light. Whether through an act of kindness, a word of encouragement, or a moment of patience, let your actions reflect His love.

Day 17: Speaking of What We Have Seen

"For we cannot help speaking about what we have seen and heard." — Acts 4:20

Peter and John had just been warned by the religious leaders to stop preaching about Jesus. They were threatened, pressured, and told to stay silent. But their response was clear: *"We cannot help speaking about what we have seen and heard."*

The Resurrection was not just a belief to them—it was a reality they had witnessed firsthand. They had seen Jesus alive. They had spoken with Him, touched His scars, and watched Him ascend. There was no way they could keep quiet about it.

Our faith is meant to be the same. When we truly encounter Christ, it changes us. We don't need perfect words or deep theology—we simply share what we have seen and experienced. If Jesus has given you peace, hope, or healing, your testimony is powerful.

So why do we hesitate? Sometimes we fear rejection, or we assume people won't care. But just like Peter and John, we are not called to convince people—we are called to share what we know and let God do the rest.

What has Jesus done in your life that you can't keep to yourself?

⋯⋯⋯◆⋯⋯⋯

Lord, You have been at work
in my life in ways I cannot deny.
Give me the courage to share
Your goodness with those around me.
Help me not to fear rejection,
but to trust that my story
—however simple—is part of Your greater plan.
Amen.

⋯⋯⋯◆⋯⋯⋯

Take a moment to reflect on one way Jesus has transformed your life. Who in your life needs to hear that encouragement? Ask God for an opportunity to share it with them this week.

Day 18: The Power of Your Story

"Return to your home, and declare how much God has done for you." And he went away, proclaiming throughout the whole city how much Jesus had done for him. — Luke 8:39

After Jesus healed a man who had been tormented for years, the man wanted nothing more than to stay with Him. But Jesus had another plan—He sent him home to tell his story.

Jesus didn't ask him to memorize Scripture, prepare a sermon, or become an expert in theology. He simply told him to share what God had done. And that testimony changed lives.

Your story has power, too. Maybe you think it's not dramatic enough or that you don't know how to explain it well. But witnessing isn't about having the perfect words—it's about being real about the ways Jesus has transformed your life.

There are people in your life who need to hear what God has done for you. Your struggles, your victories, your moments of grace—all of it is part of a greater story that God is writing, and He can use it to bring others closer to Him.

Who in your life needs to hear how Jesus has worked in your heart?

Jesus, thank You for all that
You have done in my life.
Give me the courage to share my story,
trusting that You can use even
my smallest testimony to bring hope to others.
Help me to be bold in proclaiming Your goodness.
Amen.

Think of one way Jesus has changed your life. Write it down as if you were sharing it with a friend. Ask God for an opportunity to tell someone how He has worked in you.

Day 19: Faith in Action

"Dear children, let us not love with words or speech but with actions and in truth." — 1 John 3:18

Words can be powerful, but they are empty if they are not backed by action. John reminds us that our faith is not just something we speak—it's something we live. Jesus didn't just talk about love; He demonstrated it in everything He did, from healing the sick to washing the feet of His disciples.

As witnesses of the Resurrection, our actions should reflect the love we have received. This doesn't mean grand gestures or public displays—it means choosing daily to serve, to give, to love without expecting anything in return.

Sometimes, the most powerful testimony isn't what we say but how we live. The way we treat people, our kindness in difficult moments, our willingness to forgive—these things speak louder than words.

Who in your life needs to see Christ's love through your actions today?

Lord,
help me to live out my faith
in a way that reflects Your love.
Let my actions speak of Your grace and truth,
so that others may see You through me.
Give me the strength to love,
serve, and give as You did.
Amen.

Be intentional about showing Christ's love today. Look for a small but meaningful way to serve someone—whether through kindness, generosity, or encouragement.

Day 20: The Courage to Stand Firm

"Be on your guard; stand firm in the faith; be courageous; be strong." — 1 Corinthians 16:13

Being a witness for Christ isn't always easy. The disciples faced opposition, ridicule, and even persecution, yet they refused to stay silent. They had seen the risen Jesus, and nothing could shake their faith.

We may not face the same dangers they did, but we will encounter moments where standing firm in our faith requires courage. Maybe it's speaking up when it's easier to stay quiet, choosing integrity when compromise is expected, or holding onto hope when the world around us feels hopeless.

True faith isn't just believing in Jesus—it's living for Him, even when it costs us something. The good news is that we don't have to do it alone. God strengthens those who trust in Him. He gives us the courage we need to stand firm, just as He did for the first disciples.

Where in your life is God calling you to stand firm today?

Lord,
give me the courage to stand firm in my faith,
even when it's difficult.
Help me to trust that You are my strength
and that You will equip me for every challenge.
Let my life reflect
the unshakable hope of the Resurrection.
Amen.

———◆O◆———

Think of an area in your life where it's hard to stand firm in your faith. Ask God for boldness, and take one small step today to live courageously for Him.

Day 21: A Life That Points to Christ

"He must become greater; I must become less." — John 3:30

John the Baptist had spent his life preparing the way for Jesus. People followed him, respected him, and listened to his words. But when Jesus began His ministry, John didn't hold onto the spotlight. Instead, he said, "He must become greater; I must become less."

This is the heart of being a witness. Our lives are not about making a name for ourselves but about pointing others to Christ. The way we live, the way we love, the way we serve—all of it should reflect His greatness, not our own.

It's easy to get caught up in wanting recognition, approval, or praise. But true joy comes when we surrender those desires and let Jesus take center stage. The more we focus on Him, the more our lives naturally become a testimony to His goodness.

Does your life point others to Jesus? Are there areas where you are still trying to hold onto control, recognition, or personal success instead of letting Him be glorified?

———◆○◆———

Jesus,
I want my life to reflect You.
Help me to let go of anything that
keeps me from pointing others to You.
Teach me to live in humility,
with a heart that desires
Your glory above my own. Amen.

———◆○◆———

Do something today that serves or encourages someone else—without seeking recognition or thanks. Let your actions quietly point to Christ.

MY NOTES

MY NOTES

CHAPTER FOUR

Week 4 – Strength in Trials

TRUSTING CHRIST IN DIFFICULTIES

T he Resurrection does not promise a life without trials, but it does promise that we never face them alone.

This week, we confront the reality of suffering through the lens of Christ's victory. Challenges will come, but they do not have the final word. In every struggle, every uncertainty, and every moment of weakness, God's strength is at work in us. The cross was not the end of Jesus' story, and this trial is not the end of yours.

———◆———

Day 22: When Trials Test Your Faith

"Consider it pure joy, my brothers and sisters, whenever you face trials of many kinds, because you know that the testing of your faith produces perseverance." — James 1:2-3

Faith is easy when life is smooth, but what happens when trials come? James challenges us with a radical perspective—to see difficulties as opportunities for growth, not obstacles to avoid.

Trials refine us, stripping away self-reliance and deepening our trust in God. Just as fire strengthens gold, our faith is made stronger not in ease, but in endurance. Jesus Himself endured suffering before glory, showing us that God's greatest work often happens in our hardest moments.

If you're facing a struggle today, know this: God is using it to shape you, not break you.

───────◆───────

Father,
when trials come,
help me to trust instead of doubt,
to endure instead of retreat.
Strengthen my faith
and remind me that You are working,
even in the struggle. Amen.

───────◆───────

Take a moment to reflect on a current challenge. Instead of asking "Why me?" ask, "What is God teaching me?" Write down one way this trial could be deepening your faith.

Day 23: God's Strength in Your Weakness

"My grace is sufficient for you, for my power is made perfect in weakness." — 2 Corinthians 12:9

Weakness is something we try to hide, avoid, or overcome. But God sees it differently. Where we feel inadequate, He sees an opportunity for His strength to be revealed.

Paul pleaded with God to remove his suffering, but instead of taking it away, God gave him something greater—grace that was enough. The Resurrection proves that even in the darkest moments, God's power is at work. What feels like failure or limitation to us is often the very place where God is moving.

You don't have to be strong all the time. You just need to lean on the One who is.

Lord,
I surrender my weakness to You.
Teach me to rely on Your strength
instead of my own.
Let my struggles become a testimony

of Your power at work in me.

Amen.

What area of your life feels like a weakness right now? Instead of fighting against it, ask God to meet you in it. Write a simple prayer inviting Him into that struggle.

Day 24: He Is with You in the Storm

"Then he got up and rebuked the winds and the waves, and it was completely calm." — Matthew 8:26

The disciples had seen Jesus perform miracles, yet when a storm threatened their boat, fear took over. In their panic, they forgot who was with them. But Jesus was not worried. He stood, spoke, and the storm obeyed.

Storms in life come suddenly—unexpected challenges, disappointments, or seasons of uncertainty. In those moments, it's easy to focus on the waves, to feel overwhelmed and afraid. But Jesus has not left the boat. He is still in control, still speaking peace, still reminding us: *"Why are you afraid? I am here."*

No matter what storm you face, you are not alone. His presence is greater than the waves.

Jesus,

when the storms of life shake me,

remind me that You are near.

Help me to trust that You are

greater than my fears

and that Your peace is stronger

than the chaos around me.

Amen.

———◆———

What "storm" are you facing today? Instead of focusing on the problem, take a deep breath and pray: *"Jesus, I trust You."* Let His presence bring peace.

Day 25: When You Don't Understand

"Trust in the Lord with all your heart and lean not on your own understanding." — Proverbs 3:5

Some trials don't make sense. We pray, we seek answers, and yet we are met with silence. In those moments, it's tempting to question God, to wonder why He allows certain struggles, or to feel like He is distant.

But faith is not about having all the answers—it's about trusting the One who does. The Resurrection itself was a mystery beyond human understanding. The disciples were confused, afraid, uncertain. But God's plan was unfolding, even when they couldn't see it.

You may not understand what God is doing in this moment, but you can trust that He is working for your good. Faith is choosing to lean on Him even when the path is unclear.

Lord,
I don't need to understand everything
to trust You.
Help me to let go of my need for control
and to rest in the assurance
that You are leading me,
even in uncertainty.
Amen.

Is there a situation in your life where you are struggling to understand God's plan? Write it down, and instead of asking *"Why?"* pray, *"God, help me to trust You through this."*

Day 26: The Refiner's Fire

"These trials will show that your faith is genuine. It is being tested as fire tests and purifies gold—though your faith is far more precious than mere gold." — 1 Peter 1:7 (NLT)

Fire refines gold, burning away impurities to make it stronger and more valuable. Peter tells us that our faith is tested the same way—not to break us, but to purify us.

Trials reveal what we truly believe. They strip away shallow faith and invite us to trust God more deeply. While suffering is never easy, it has a purpose: to strengthen, refine, and draw us closer to Him. The Resurrection itself came after the greatest trial of all—the cross. If God could bring victory from suffering then, He can do the same in your life now.

You may not see the purpose in your trial yet, but God is refining you through it. Trust that what He is doing in you is worth far more than gold.

Lord,
I may not always understand the trials I face,
but I trust that You
are refining me through them.
Strengthen my faith
and help me to see
that You are at work,
even in the fire. Amen.

Think of a past trial that, in hindsight, helped shape your faith. How did God use it for good? Write it down as a reminder that He is working in your current struggles, too.

Day 27: His Strength, Not Yours

"The Lord is my strength and my shield; my heart trusts in him, and he helps me." — Psalm 28:7

Some days, we feel strong. Other days, we don't. Life's challenges can drain us—physically, emotionally, spiritually. But the good news is that our strength was never meant to come from us.

David, a mighty warrior and king, didn't boast in his own power—he declared that the Lord was his strength and shield. The same is true for us. God never asks us to carry our burdens alone. He invites us to trust Him, lean on Him, and draw from His unlimited strength.

If you feel weary today, know this: you don't have to be enough—because He is.

———◆○◆———

Father,
when I feel weak,
remind me that Your strength is always enough.
Teach me to trust You
instead of relying on my own abilities.
Be my shield, my help,
and my source of strength today.
Amen.

———◆○◆———

If you are feeling weary today, pause and pray: "*Lord, I need Your strength.*" Then take a practical step to rest—whether through prayer, worship, or simply taking a moment of stillness with Him.

Day 28: Victory Through Christ

"But thanks be to God! He gives us the victory through our Lord Jesus Christ." — 1 Corinthians 15:57

Every trial, every struggle, every moment of uncertainty is met with this truth: the victory has already been won. We do not fight for victory; we fight from victory—the victory of Christ.

When Jesus walked out of the grave, He declared that death, sin, and suffering do not have the final say. No matter what you are facing, no matter how overwhelming it feels, you are not defeated. You are standing in the victory of Christ.

This doesn't mean that life will be without hardship, but it does mean that hardship will never have the last word. The empty tomb is proof that God's power is greater than anything that comes against you. Hold onto that truth today—you are walking in victory, not defeat.

———◄O►———

Jesus,
thank You for the victory
You have won for me.
When trials come,

help me to stand firm in the truth
that You have already overcome.
Let my faith rest in Your finished work,
not in my own strength.
Amen.

Speak victory over your life today. Instead of focusing on what feels overwhelming, declare: "Through Christ, I have victory." Let that truth shape how you approach today's challenges.

MY NOTES

MY NOTES

CHAPTER FIVE

Week 5 – Preparing for the Spirit

OPENING OUR HEARTS TO PENTECOST

T he Resurrection was just the beginning. Jesus didn't rise only to leave us as we were—He rose to prepare us for something greater.

Before ascending to heaven, He told His disciples to wait for the promise of the Father—the Holy Spirit. The same Spirit that raised Christ from the dead was about to dwell within them, empowering them to live, speak, and move in His power.

This week, we turn our hearts toward that promise. Are we ready to receive all that God wants to give? The Spirit is not just for the first disciples—it is for us. For today. For the life we are called to live. Are we making room for Him?

Day 30: A Heart Ready to Receive

"I will give you a new heart and put a new spirit in you; I will remove from you your heart of stone and give you a heart of flesh." — Ezekiel 36:26

The Holy Spirit is always ready to fill us, to guide us, to move in us. But are we ready to receive Him?

Sometimes, we hold back. We resist change, cling to control, or let doubt cloud our faith. But God's promise is clear: He desires to give us a new heart, one that is soft and open to His Spirit.

Just as dry ground cannot absorb water, a hardened heart cannot fully receive what God wants to pour out. But when we surrender, when we let go of fear and resistance, He does what only He can—He transforms us from within.

What is keeping your heart from being fully open to the Spirit?

———— ◆ ————

Lord, soften my heart.
Remove anything that keeps me
from fully receiving Your Spirit.
Make me open, ready, and willing
for whatever You want to do in me.
Amen.

Ask God to reveal anything in your heart that is resisting Him—fear, doubt, distraction. Spend time in prayer, surrendering it to Him.

Day 31: The Spirit as Our Helper

"And I will ask the Father, and he will give you another Helper, to be with you forever." — John 14:16

Jesus knew that His disciples would feel lost without Him. They had walked beside Him, listened to His voice, and relied on His presence. But He promised them something incredible—a Helper who would never leave them.

The Holy Spirit is not just a force or a feeling; He is our constant companion, our guide, our strength. He speaks when we need wisdom, comforts when we feel weak, and empowers us when we feel unworthy.

You are not alone in your journey of faith. The same Spirit that Jesus promised His disciples is alive in you today. Are you relying on Him, or are you trying to walk this path on your own?

Holy Spirit,
thank You for being my Helper.

Remind me that
I don't have to rely on my own strength,
because You are always with me.
Teach me to listen, to trust,
and to walk in step with You. Amen.

———◦———

Before making any decision today—big or small—pause and pray: *"Holy Spirit, guide me."* Be mindful of His presence as you go through your day.

Day 32: The Spirit Gives Life

*"The Spirit gives life; the flesh counts for nothing. The words
I have spoken to you—they are full of the Spirit and life."* —
John 6:63

Life in Christ is not just about following rules or striving to be better—it is about being filled with the Spirit. Without Him, faith can feel like a struggle, a constant effort to do what is right. But Jesus reminds us that it is the Spirit who gives life.

The same Spirit that breathed life into creation, that raised Jesus from the dead, is the One who renews and strengthens us today. He fills what is empty, revives what feels dry, and restores what is broken.

If you've been feeling weary in your faith, remember this: God never intended for you to do this alone. His Spirit is the source of life, and He is always ready to fill you.

———◄O►———

Lord,
breathe Your life into me.
Refresh my soul, restore my passion for You,
and renew my heart.
Let Your Spirit awaken me
to the fullness of life
that only You can give.
Amen.

———◄O►———

Take five minutes today to sit in stillness. Breathe deeply and pray, *"Holy Spirit, fill me with Your life."* Let His presence renew you.

Day 33: Led by the Spirit

"For those who are led by the Spirit of God are the children of God." — Romans 8:14

Walking with Christ is not about knowing every step in advance—it's about trusting the One who leads. The Holy Spirit is our guide, not just in big life decisions, but in the everyday moments where faith meets action.

Being led by the Spirit means learning to listen, trust, and follow, even when we don't have all the answers. Sometimes, His leading comes as a gentle nudge, a sense of peace, or an unexpected opportunity. Other times, it's a call to let go of control and step forward in faith.

The more we open our hearts to the Spirit, the clearer His voice becomes. Are you letting Him lead, or are you trying to figure it out on your own?

———◦———

Holy Spirit,
I want to be led by You.
Help me to recognize Your voice,
to trust Your direction,
and to follow wherever You lead me.
Let my life be guided
by Your wisdom, not my own.
Amen.

———◦———

Before making a decision today, big or small, pause and pray: "*Holy Spirit, lead me.*" Pay attention to how He directs your heart.

Day 34: The Spirit of Peace

"The mind governed by the Spirit is life and peace." — Romans 8:6

True peace isn't found in perfect circumstances—it's found in God's presence. The world offers temporary relief, but the Holy Spirit gives a lasting peace that is not shaken by fear, uncertainty, or trials.

When we allow the Spirit to guide our minds, our hearts become anchored in Christ, no matter what storms come our way. His peace is not about ignoring difficulties but about knowing that we are held, secure, and never alone.

If anxiety, stress, or worry have been filling your heart, turn to the Spirit. His peace is already within you—you just need to receive it.

———◆———

Holy Spirit,
fill me with Your peace.
Quiet the noise of my worries
and remind me that You are in control.
Let my heart and mind
rest in Your presence today. Amen.

———◆———

If anxiety creeps in today, pause and take a deep breath. Pray: *"Holy Spirit, I choose Your peace over my fear."* Let that truth settle in your heart.

Day 35: The Spirit Prepares Us

"But the Advocate, the Holy Spirit, whom the Father will send
in my name, will teach you all things and will remind you of
everything I have said to you." — John 14:26

Before Pentecost, the disciples were waiting—but they were not waiting alone. Jesus had already prepared them for what was coming. He promised that the Holy Spirit would be their Advocate, their Teacher, their Reminder of everything He had spoken.

The Spirit still works the same way today. He prepares our hearts, equips us for what's ahead, and brings God's truth to mind exactly when we need it. Whether we are stepping into new challenges, facing uncertainties, or feeling unready, we can trust that God has already given us everything we need through His Spirit.

You don't have to rely on your own wisdom or strength—the Spirit is guiding you, teaching you, and preparing you for what's next. Are you listening?

———◄O►———

Father,
prepare my heart for what
You are doing in my life.
Teach me, guide me, and remind me
of the truth of Christ.
Help me to trust that You are equipping me
for what's ahead. Amen.

———◄O►———

Ask God to prepare your heart for Pentecost. Take a moment today to pray: *"Holy Spirit, teach me what I need to know and remind me of what I need to remember."*

Day 36: Filled with the Spirit

"Do not get drunk on wine, which leads to debauchery. Instead, be filled with the Spirit." — Ephesians 5:18

Pentecost is near, and with it comes the invitation to be filled with the Holy Spirit. Paul's words remind us that this is not a one-time event, but a continuous experience—a life led and empowered by God's presence.

To be "filled" with the Spirit means yielding to His work in us, allowing Him to shape our thoughts, actions, and desires. It means living with an open heart, ready to receive more of His presence every day. The question is not whether God is willing to fill us—the question is whether we are making room for Him.

What areas of your life still need to be surrendered to the Spirit?

———— ◄O► ————

Lord,
I desire to be filled with Your Spirit.
Remove anything in me
that resists Your presence,
and help me to live fully led by You.
Let my heart remain open

to Your power and guidance every day.

Amen.

Spend a few quiet moments inviting the Holy Spirit into your heart. Pray: *"Lord, fill me anew today."* Be still, and listen for His presence.

MY NOTES

MY NOTES

CHAPTER SIX

Week 6 – Living in the Spirit

TRANSFORMATION THROUGH THE HOLY SPIRIT

The gift of the Holy Spirit wasn't given for a single moment, but for a lifetime. When the disciples received Him at Pentecost, everything changed. Fear gave way to boldness, hesitation turned into action, and their faith was no longer just belief—it was power in motion.

The same Spirit dwells in us today, renewing, guiding, and strengthening. He is not distant or occasional but present in every step we take. Learning to live in the Spirit means embracing His leading, trusting His voice, and allowing Him to shape our daily lives.

This week is about walking in that transformation. The Spirit is already at work—are we making space for Him to move?

———◦○◦———

Day 37: Walking in the Spirit

"So I say, walk by the Spirit, and you will not gratify the desires of the flesh." — Galatians 5:16

Faith is not just about believing—it's about walking. Paul reminds us that the Christian life is not meant to be powered by our own strength, but by the Spirit leading us every step of the way.

Walking in the Spirit means learning to listen, trust, and follow rather than relying on our own understanding. It's a daily choice to align our thoughts, decisions, and actions with God's will instead of being pulled by selfish desires or fears.

The Spirit is already at work in you. Are you moving with Him, or are you still trying to lead the way?

———◆———

Holy Spirit,
guide my steps today.
Help me to recognize
when I am trying to walk
in my own strength
and to surrender instead to Your leading.
Teach me to trust and follow You.
Amen.

———◆O◆———

Be intentional today about inviting the Spirit into your decisions. Before reacting, responding, or making a choice, pause and ask: *"Holy Spirit, what do You want me to do?"*

Day 38: Led by the Spirit

"Since we live by the Spirit, let us keep in step with the Spirit."
— Galatians 5:25

Life in the Spirit is more than a moment of inspiration—it's a rhythm, a way of moving through the world in harmony with God's leading. Paul's words remind us that being filled with the Spirit is not just about having Him within us, but about staying in step with Him.

Keeping in step means learning to recognize His voice, to slow down when He calls us to wait, and to move forward when He prompts us to act. It's about responding to His presence rather than rushing ahead on our own.

The Spirit is always leading—are you staying in step?

———◆O◆———

Lord,
teach me to walk at Your pace.
Help me to listen when You speak,

to wait when You call me to be still,

and to move when You lead.

Keep my heart in tune with Your Spirit today.

Amen.

———◆◇◆———

Take a few moments to pause throughout your day. Before moving to your next task, pray: *"Holy Spirit, am I in step with You?"* Listen for His direction.

Day 39: The Spirit Renews Our Minds

"Do not conform to the pattern of this world, but be trans-formed by the renewing of your mind." — Romans 12:2

The way we think shapes the way we live. Paul reminds us that true transformation begins not with outward change, but with the renewal of our minds. The Holy Spirit is constantly at work, reshaping our thoughts, correcting our perspectives, and aligning our hearts with God's truth.

It's easy to be influenced by the world's way of thinking—fears, doubts, selfish ambitions—but the Spirit invites us to something higher. He fills our minds with truth, wisdom, and peace, replacing confusion with clarity and fear with faith.

What thoughts are shaping your life today? Are they guided by the Spirit or by the world?

———◆◇◆———

Holy Spirit,
renew my mind.
Remove any thoughts that pull me away from You,
and fill me with truth that leads to life.
Teach me to see the world through Your perspective.
Amen.

———◆◇◆———

Pay attention to your thoughts today. If you notice worry, doubt, or negativity creeping in, pause and pray: *"Holy Spirit, renew my mind with Your truth."*

Day 40: The Fruit of the Spirit

"But the fruit of the Spirit is love, joy, peace, forbearance, kindness, goodness, faithfulness, gentleness and self-control." — Galatians 5:22-23

A tree doesn't struggle to bear fruit—it produces naturally when it is healthy and connected to its source of life. The same is true for us. When we walk with the Spirit, His presence in us naturally produces His fruit.

Love, joy, peace, and the rest of these qualities are not things we force or manufacture. They grow as a result of being rooted in God. Instead of striving to "be better," we are called to stay connected—to allow the Spirit to shape us from within.

Are you seeing His fruit in your life? If not, where might God be calling you to draw closer to Him?

Father,
let my life bear the fruit of Your Spirit.
Help me to stay connected to You
so that love, joy, and peace
flow naturally from my heart.
Shape me into the person
You created me to be.
Amen.

Choose one fruit of the Spirit that you want to grow in. Ask God to help you nurture it today, not by striving, but by staying close to Him.

Day 41: Listening to the Spirit

"Whether you turn to the right or to the left, your ears will hear a voice behind you, saying, 'This is the way; walk in it.'"
— Isaiah 30:21

God is always speaking, but are we listening? The Holy Spirit is our guide, gently leading us in the right direction, yet the noise of life can drown out His voice. Distractions, worries, and our own plans can make it hard to hear what He is saying.

Listening to the Spirit requires stillness, awareness, and trust. Sometimes He speaks through Scripture, sometimes through a gentle conviction in our hearts, and other times through people or circumstances around us. The more we listen, the clearer His voice becomes.

Have you made space to hear Him today?

———⊶◦⊷———

Holy Spirit,
help me to recognize Your voice.
Quiet the distractions that keep me
from hearing You.
Teach me to listen with an open heart
and to follow where You lead.
Amen.

———⊶◦⊷———

Take five minutes of silence today. No phone, no music—just quiet. Ask, "Holy Spirit, what do You want to say to me?" Pay attention to any thoughts or impressions that come to mind.

Day 42: Strengthened by the Spirit

"I pray that out of his glorious riches he may strengthen you with power through his Spirit in your inner being." — Ephesians 3:16

Life can feel overwhelming at times. Challenges drain our energy, and even our faith can feel weak. But Paul reminds us that true strength does not come from within us—it comes from the Spirit within us.

God never intended for us to rely on our own power. The Holy Spirit strengthens us in ways we cannot explain, giving us endurance in trials, courage in uncertainty, and peace in the midst of chaos. His power is not just for extraordinary moments—it is for everyday life.

Are you relying on your own strength, or are you drawing from the Spirit's power?

———◆◇◆———

Father, I need Your strength.
Fill me with Your Spirit
so that I can walk in Your power,
not my own.
Strengthen my heart, renew my faith, and help me
trust in Your mighty presence within me. Amen.

———◆◇◆———

The next time you feel weary today, stop and pray: *"Holy Spirit, give me strength."* Let His power renew you.

Day 43: Empowered to Shine

"You will receive power when the Holy Spirit comes on you; and you will be my witnesses in Jerusalem, and in all Judea and Samaria, and to the ends of the earth." — Acts 1:8

The Holy Spirit doesn't just transform us from within—He empowers us to make an impact. When the disciples received the Spirit at Pentecost, they didn't stay where they were. They went out, boldly proclaiming Christ, filled with a courage they had never known before.

God's Spirit in you is not meant to stay hidden. He has given you gifts, wisdom, and strength—not for your benefit alone, but so that His light may shine through you. Where is He calling you to step out in faith?

The same power that filled the first disciples is alive in you today. Are you ready to walk in it?

Holy Spirit,
empower me to be a witness for Christ.
Remove my fear, fill me with boldness,
and use me to bring
Your love and truth into the world.
Let Your power shine through my life.
Amen.

Ask God to show you one way you can step out in faith today. It could be an act of kindness, a word of encouragement, or sharing your testimony. Trust that He will equip you.

MY NOTES

MY NOTES

CHAPTER SEVEN

Week 7 – The Mission of Pentecost

LIVING BOLDLY FOR CHRIST

Pentecost was not the end of a season—it was the beginning of the Church's mission. The disciples, once hesitant and unsure, stepped forward with boldness, power, and purpose, carrying the message of Christ to the world.

The same Spirit that filled them at Pentecost fills us today. We are not meant to keep our faith to ourselves but to live it out fearlessly, sharing the love and truth of Jesus in every place He leads us.

This week, we step into our mission. The Spirit is moving—are we ready to go where He sends us?

Day 44: Sent with Purpose

"Again Jesus said, 'Peace be with you! As the Father has sent me, I am sending you.'" — John 20:21

Jesus didn't just call His disciples to follow Him—He sent them into the world. The resurrection wasn't the end of their journey; it was the beginning of their mission.

That same calling extends to us. We are not meant to live a passive faith but an active one—a life that reflects Christ, shares His love, and carries His truth wherever we go. The Holy Spirit equips us, strengthens us, and leads us, but we must be willing to step forward.

Where is God sending you? Maybe it's into a conversation, an act of kindness, or simply a deeper commitment to living out your faith. Wherever it is, go with confidence—because Jesus goes with you.

———◄O►———

Lord,
You have called me and sent me.
Help me to embrace the mission
You have for my life.
Give me boldness, clarity, and faith
to walk where You lead.
Amen.

———◄O►———

Ask God to show you one way He is calling you to live out your faith today. Step into it with trust, knowing He has sent you.

Day 45: Boldness Through the Spirit

"After they prayed, the place where they were meeting was shaken. And they were all filled with the Holy Spirit and spoke the word of God boldly." — Acts 4:31

Fear kept the disciples in hiding after Jesus' crucifixion, but something changed at Pentecost. The Holy Spirit filled them with boldness, and they began to preach with confidence, no longer afraid of opposition.

This same boldness is available to us. The Spirit does not make us timid; He empowers us to live and speak with courage, clarity, and conviction. Sharing our faith may feel intimidating at times, but we are not alone—the Spirit gives us the words, the strength, and the confidence to proclaim Christ wherever we are.

Where is God calling you to step out in faith today? What would change if you truly believed the Spirit was empowering you?

Holy Spirit,
fill me with boldness.
Remove my fear, strengthen my faith,
and give me the courage
to speak and live for Christ.

Help me to trust that You
will give me the words when I need them.
Amen.

Do one thing today that requires spiritual boldness—whether it's sharing your faith, praying for someone, or stepping into a new opportunity God is calling you to. Trust that the Spirit will equip you.

Day 46: Being a Light in the World

"You are the light of the world. A city on a hill cannot be hidden." — Matthew 5:14

Jesus didn't say one day we might become the light of the world—He said we already are. The presence of the Holy Spirit within us is meant to shine, not be hidden.

Our lives should reflect Christ in a way that draws others to Him—not through perfection, but through love, kindness, and the hope we carry. The world is filled with uncertainty and darkness, but God has placed His Spirit in us to be beacons of His truth, peace, and grace.

The question is not whether we have the light—it's whether we are willing to let it shine. Are you living in a way that points others to Jesus?

Lord,

let my life reflect Your light.

Help me to shine with Your love,

to bring hope where there is darkness,

and to live in a way that glorifies You.

Amen.

———————◀◆▶———————

Be intentional about shining Christ's light today. Show kindness, extend grace, or speak encouragement to someone who needs it.

Day 47: Equipped for Every Good Work

"May the God of peace... equip you with everything good for doing his will, and may he work in us what is pleasing to him, through Jesus Christ." — Hebrews 13:20-21

God never calls us without also equipping us. The Holy Spirit provides everything we need to carry out the work He has set before us. We may feel unprepared, weak, or unsure, but our confidence does not come from our abilities—it comes from His power at work within us.

The Spirit is not just present for moments of worship or prayer; He is with us in the ordinary, equipping us for the conversations we'll have, the decisions we'll make, and the love we're called to show. Every moment is an opportunity to rely on Him.

Where in your life do you need to trust that God has already equipped you?

Father,
thank You for equipping me
for every good work.
Help me to trust that You
have already given me
what I need to fulfill Your purpose.
Strengthen my faith and remind me
that I am never walking alone.
Amen.

Step into today with confidence. Whatever challenge or opportunity comes your way, pause and remind yourself: *"God has already equipped me for this."*

Day 48: Speaking with Grace and Truth

"Let your conversation be always full of grace, seasoned with salt, so that you may know how to answer everyone." — Colossians 4:6

The way we speak matters. Our words have the power to build up or tear down, to bring hope or spread doubt. Paul reminds us that when we speak, it should be with grace and wisdom, reflecting the love and truth of Christ.

Living in the Spirit means allowing Him to shape not just our actions but also our words. Whether in conversations with family, coworkers, or strangers, we are called to speak in a way that draws people toward God, not away from Him.

Do your words today reflect the presence of the Spirit in your life?

———◦———

Holy Spirit,
guide my words.
Help me to speak with grace, kindness,
and truth, so that my conversations
reflect Your love.
Teach me when to speak and when to listen.
Amen.

———◦———

Be intentional about your words today. Before responding in a conversation, pause and ask: *"Is this full of grace? Is this leading others toward Christ?"*

Day 49: A Life of Surrender

"I have been crucified with Christ and I no longer live, but Christ lives in me." — Galatians 2:20

The Christian life is not about control—it's about surrender. Paul's words remind us that when we belong to Christ, we are no longer the center of our own story. The Spirit leads, and we follow.

Surrender is not about weakness; it is about trusting that God's plan is greater than our own. The more we let go of fear, doubt, and the need to control, the more room we make for the Holy Spirit to move in our lives.

What are you holding onto that God is asking you to release?

———— ◆◇◆ ————

Lord,
I surrender my plans, my fears,
and my desires to You.
Let my life be fully Yours.
Teach me to trust Your leading,
knowing that Christ lives in me.
Amen.

———— ◆◇◆ ————

Ask God to reveal an area of your life where you need to surrender. Write it down, pray over it, and commit to trusting Him with it today.

MY NOTES

MY NOTES

CHAPTER EIGHT

Pentecost

THE FULFILLMENT OF THE PROMISE

P entecost marks the moment when God's promise was fulfilled—the Holy Spirit was poured out, and everything changed. The disciples had been waiting, gathered in prayer, uncertain of what was to come. Then, heaven moved.

> *"When the day of Pentecost came, they were all together in one place. Suddenly a sound like the blowing of a violent wind came from heaven and filled the whole house where they were sitting. They saw what seemed to be tongues of fire that separated and came to rest on each of them. All of them were filled with the Holy Spirit and began to speak in other tongues as the Spirit enabled them." — Acts 2:1-4*

Wind and fire—symbols of God's power and presence—swept through the room. The Spirit didn't come quietly; He arrived with a force that could not be ignored. In that instant, the disciples were filled, transformed, and sent into the world with a mission that would never fade.

From that day forward, their lives were no longer shaped by fear but by boldness, power, and purpose. This was the beginning of the Church, the start of something unstoppable.

The same Spirit continues His work today, equipping, leading, and empowering. Are we making space for Him to move?

The Moment That Changed Everything

For weeks, the disciples had waited, gathered in prayer as Jesus had instructed. They knew a promise was coming, but they didn't know when or how it would arrive. Then, Pentecost changed everything.

The Spirit didn't come as a gentle whisper. He arrived with power—wind that shook the room and fire that rested upon them. In an instant, these ordinary men and women were filled with a strength beyond themselves. Fear disappeared. Boldness took its place. The ones who had once scattered at Jesus' arrest now stood before the crowds, proclaiming His name without hesitation.

This was the turning point. No longer just followers, the disciples became witnesses, preachers, and pioneers of a movement that would reach the ends of the earth. Their message was no longer just words—it was Spirit-empowered truth that transformed hearts and lives.

Pentecost was not an isolated event in history. The Spirit didn't come for a single moment—He came to dwell, to empower, and to lead. His presence is just as real today as it was in that upper room. The same power that ignited the disciples is available to us.

Are we living in the fullness of what God has given? Have we embraced the Spirit's power, or are we still waiting on the sidelines?

The Spirit's Role: Then and Now

The Holy Spirit didn't just descend on Pentecost to mark an occasion—He came to transform lives and launch the mission of the Church. His role wasn't temporary; He continues to work today just as He did then.

At Pentecost, He empowered the disciples to speak boldly, gave them words they couldn't have formed on their own, and filled them with courage that overcame fear. The Spirit was not just an external force—He dwelled within them, making their bodies His temple and their lives His witness.

That same Spirit lives in every believer today. He teaches, convicts, strengthens, and guides. He is the voice that speaks truth when confusion clouds our minds, the comforter who brings peace when fear creeps in, and the power that enables us to do what we could never accomplish on our own.

Many times, we live as though we have to rely on our own strength, struggling to figure things out on our own. But the Spirit is not distant—He is present, willing, and ready to lead us. He is not limited to the early Church or to great spiritual leaders—He is for all who call on Christ.

The question is not whether the Holy Spirit is at work—the question is, are we allowing Him to move freely in our lives?

Prayer of Surrender & Renewal

Holy Spirit,
I open my heart to You today.

Just as You filled the disciples at Pentecost, fill me anew.
Remove any hesitation, any fear, any resistance within me.
Let Your fire ignite my faith,
and let Your wind move me where You will.

I don't want to live by my own strength
—I want to live fully empowered by You.
Lead me, teach me, and remind me that I am never alone.
Transform my heart, my thoughts, and my actions
so that my life reflects the power of Your presence.

Come, Holy Spirit.
I am Yours. Amen.

Stepping into the Mission

Pentecost was not the end—it was the beginning. The Spirit didn't come just to inspire; He came to send, empower, and equip. The same is true today. The work of the Kingdom continues, and we are part of it.

The question is, how will you respond?

- Invite the Holy Spirit to lead you today. Pray, "Holy Spirit, show me where You are calling me to step out in faith."

- Look for an opportunity to be bold. Whether it's sharing your faith, showing kindness, or stepping into a new responsibility, trust that He will equip you.

- Walk in expectation. The Spirit is already at work in you. Live today with confidence, knowing you are empowered for a purpose.

Pentecost was the spark that set the Church in motion. That fire is still burning. Will you carry it forward?

MY NOTES

MY NOTES

CHAPTER NINE

Living in the Light Beyond Pentecost

A GUIDE TO PRAYER AND MEDITATION FOR CONTINUING THE JOURNEY

"Since we live by the Spirit, let us keep in step with the Spirit."
— Galatians 5:25

P entecost marks the end of the 50-day journey, but it is not the end of transformation. It is a launching point, a moment when the Holy Spirit empowers us to step forward with renewed faith. The challenge is not just to receive the Spirit but to continue walking in His presence, allowing Him to shape our lives beyond this season.

Too often, we experience spiritual renewal only to find ourselves slipping back into old routines. The fire that once burned brightly can fade if we do not tend to it. But Jesus did not send the Holy Spirit for a temporary revival—He sent Him to be our constant companion, guiding us in every step of our daily lives.

To sustain the renewal we've experienced, we must actively nurture our connection with God. How do we keep the spiritual momentum alive? How do we remain open to the Spirit's leading beyond Pentecost? The answer lies in intentionality. Faith must be cultivated, like a garden that flourishes only when it is watered and cared for.

This chapter offers practical ways to stay connected to the Spirit, to deepen our relationship with God, and to carry the light of Christ into every part of our lives.

The Call to Keep Walking in the Light

After experiencing the uplifting spirit of Easter, it might feel natural to slip back into our everyday patterns. Yet, such profound spiritual renewal isn't meant to be boxed away until next Easter. Pentecost isn't just a final point on the church calendar—it signals a continuation, a beckoning to carry this renewed faith into every part of our lives daily.

You might wonder, *"How do I prevent this spiritual high from just fading away?"* It's about weaving this renewed faith into your daily decisions and interactions, ensuring that this isn't just a seasonal change but a new way to approach life year-round.

Consider this: Galatians 5:16 encourages us, *"Walk by the Spirit, and you will not gratify the desires of the flesh."* It's a reminder that living by the Spirit isn't just for moments of high religious observance but for every moment of our lives. By choosing each day to walk in the light of the Spirit, we can resist slipping back into old habits that don't reflect our spiritual growth.

So, how can you keep this momentum going? It starts with a conscious decision to integrate your faith deeply and actively, not compartmentalizing it to certain times or places. It's about choosing a path where spiritual decisions shape everyday actions, continually renewing your commitment to walk by the Spirit.

Are you ready to embrace this daily challenge and carry the joy and lessons of Easter into every day? Let's explore practical ways to live out this commitment, ensuring that your faith is a vibrant part of your everyday life.

Practical Ways to Cultivate a Daily Spiritual Life

Maintaining a vibrant spiritual life requires us to set rhythms that keep us connected to God throughout our daily routines. Here are some ways to cultivate such a rhythm in your life, ensuring that your spiritual renewal extends beyond special seasons and becomes a part of your everyday existence.

A. Setting a Rhythm of Prayer and Reflection

Establishing a sustainable prayer routine is foundational. Whether it's starting your day with a morning prayer or closing it with reflections in the evening, these touchpoints can serve as anchors, keeping you grounded in your faith. Consider integrating practices like Lectio Divina, a meditative reading that invites you to ponder deeply on God's Word, allowing it to speak into your life in new ways.

<u>Morning and Evening Prayers</u>

Morning Prayer: Begin each day by offering your plans to God and asking for His guidance. This sets a tone of reliance on God's will, helping you to navigate the day with a spirit-led perspective.

Evening Prayer: Reflect on your day in the presence of God. Acknowledge your successes and failures, and seek His peace and forgiveness. This helps to process the day's events through a spiritual lens, promoting peace and gratitude.

B. The Role of Community in Spiritual Growth

Faith is not meant to be lived in isolation. Staying actively engaged with your church community can provide you with support and accountability, essential for spiritual growth. Participate in Bible study groups, join church activities, or simply share your faith journey with friends from your community.

Practical ways to stay engaged with the Church after Easter:

- Join a Small Group: Small groups provide a space for shared growth, prayer, and accountability.

- Volunteer: Serving within your church or local community can reinforce your sense of purpose and connection to others.

Recognizing the Spirit's Guidance

As you deepen your daily practices, also focus on discerning the Holy Spirit's presence in your life. This involves recognizing His voice amid the noise of everyday life and making conscious choices that align with His leading.

Steps for Practicing Spiritual Discernment:

- Daily Decision Making: Before making decisions, large or small, take a moment to pray for the Holy Spirit's guidance.

- Biblical Examples: Reflect on instances in the Bible where God led His people through the Holy Spirit. These stories can offer insights and encouragement in your own journey of discernment.

Prayers and Meditations for the Journey

As we seek to continually walk in the light of Christ, incorporating prayers and meditations into our daily lives becomes a vital practice. These spiritual tools not only enhance our connection to God but also guide us in maintaining the spiritual momentum we've cultivated.

Prayer for the Spirit's Guidance

Inspired by Solomon's request for a discerning heart in 1 Kings 3:9, this prayer seeks wisdom and clarity from the Holy Spirit:

Heavenly Father,
just as Solomon sought wisdom to govern your people,
I seek your guidance in every aspect of my life.
Grant me a discerning heart that I may recognize
your hand in the decisions I face each day.
Lead me in your ways and fill my heart
with your truth and wisdom. Amen.

Prayer to Walk in Christ's Light

Drawing from the words of Jesus in John 8:12,

"I am the light of the world...,"

this prayer is a commitment to live out the teachings of Christ in daily life:

Lord Jesus,
you declare yourself the light of the world,
a guiding beacon for all.
Illuminate my path with your divine light.
Help me to walk in your ways fearlessly,
radiating your love and truth to all I encounter.
May your light within me lead others to your grace.
Amen.

Meditation on Perseverance in Faith

Reflecting on the enduring commitment seen in 2 Timothy 4:7,

"I have fought the good fight, I have finished the race, I have kept the faith,"

this meditation focuses on the strength to persevere:

In moments of weariness and doubt,
remind me, Lord, of the race set before me.
Let me look to the saints who have persevered,
who have fought the good fight with faith unwavering.
Infuse my spirit with the same resolve,
that I may continue to serve you,
not with fleeting zeal,
but with a steadfast heart.

Small Daily Acts to Strengthen Your Faith

Embedding our daily life with simple yet profound acts of faith can transform the mundane into moments of deep spiritual growth. Each small

decision to act in faith is a step towards embodying Christ's teachings, making our daily walk with Him vibrant and alive.

Practicing Acts of Kindness

In a world that often prioritizes self-interest, choosing to perform acts of kindness is a powerful testimony of Christ's love. Whether it's helping a neighbor, offering a listening ear, or supporting a friend in need, these acts of kindness don't just change the lives of recipients—they transform our heart too, aligning us more closely with the generous spirit of Christ.

Keeping a Spiritual Journal

Maintaining a spiritual journal serves as a canvas where you can paint the landscape of your soul's journey. Documenting prayers, reflections, and answered prayers not only provides a record of your spiritual growth but also enhances your awareness of God's active presence in your life. This practice can become a source of encouragement during challenging times, reminding you of the steady hand of God guiding your path.

Participating in or Starting a Prayer Group

Communal prayer is a cornerstone of spiritual development. By joining or starting a prayer group, you create a shared space for spiritual support and accountability. This collective engagement with faith enriches your personal relationship with God and strengthens the community's bond, creating a network of faith that supports each member's spiritual growth.

Choosing a Patron Saint or Spiritual Mentor

Selecting a patron saint or a spiritual mentor can provide personal insights and guidance along your spiritual journey. These figures, whether historical saints whose lives inspire you or mentors who walk beside you, act as spiritual compasses. Their examples of faith, perseverance, and devotion offer tangible models to emulate, drawing you closer to the ideals they embody.

Conclusion: A Daily Commitment to Growth

"Let us not become weary in doing good, for at the proper time we will reap a harvest if we do not give up." — Galatians 6:9

This scripture is a compelling call to steadfastness in our spiritual endeavors. It serves as a poignant reminder that our daily efforts, those small yet significant acts of faith, are not in vain. Each step taken in kindness, every reflection penned in your journal, each prayer shared within a community, and every moment spent learning from the lives of saints and mentors, accumulates into a greater narrative of spiritual richness.

As you continue on this path, consider the profound impact of consistency in your spiritual practices. The routines we establish do not just shape our days; they form our character and deepen our relationship with God. It is in the quiet persistence, the gentle repetition of righteous acts, where true spiritual strength is forged.

Remember, growth often happens incrementally, and its fruits are not always immediately visible. However, like a tree that slowly stretches towards the sky, our souls too expand towards the divine, subtly but surely. This growth requires patience, persistence, and a heart willing to remain open and responsive to the Spirit's whispers.

As you step forward from this moment, hold onto the vision of what your steadfast faith will cultivate. Visualize the harvest that awaits from your dedication—not just for you, but for all those touched by the echoes of your faithfulness. Carry forward with the knowledge that each day is ripe with opportunities for spiritual enrichment and that each small act of faith is a building block in your life's testament to God's enduring grace.

Let this conclusion not be an end but a launching point into a life ever more reflective of Christ's love, a life that continually seeks to grow deeper and reach higher in the garden of faith you cultivate daily.

MY NOTES

MY NOTES

EXPLORE MORE FROM
THOMAS KNIGHT

Scan the QR code below to discover the entire *Inspired by Faith* series. Each book in the series offers daily reflections, prayers, and blessings to enhance your spiritual journey throughout the year.

www.chapterzerobooks.com

Made in the USA
Las Vegas, NV
23 March 2025

20010716R00066